Bluer and More Vast

D1088115

HYSTERICAL BOOKS

Bluer and More Vast

prose poems

Michael Hettich

HYSTERICAL BOOKS

TALLAHASSEE, FLORIDA 2018

Copyright © Michael Hettich   2018
All rights reserved under
International and Pan-American Copyright Conventions.

No portion of this book may be reproduced in any form without the written permission of the publisher, except by a reviewer, who may quote brief passages in connection with a review for a magazine or newspaper.

Cover Image: Carol Tadaro
Design, production: Jay Snodgrass
Type Styles: body text in Bodoni MT and titles in Futrura PT

Library of Congress Cataloging-in-Publication Data
Bluer and More Vast — First Edition
ISBN — 978-0-940821-08-8
Library of Congress Cataloging Card Number —2018946918

HYSTERICAL BOOKS
1506 Wekewa Nene
Tallahassee, Florida 32301
Website: www.hystericalbooks.com
mail: hystericalbooks@gmail.com
Published in the United States by

Hysterical Books
First Edition, 2018

for Colleen

Contents

I.

II.

III.

IV.

The emptiness of things rose like the sound of a choir making the sky bluer and more vast.

--James Salter

I.

Forgiveness

A person put together like a bundle of sticks, tied tight with twine and leaned in a corner because he or she looks beautiful there. A person swept up like sawdust on the shop floor after a day spent building sturdy furniture. Or a person imagined in the egg-filled nest abandoned in the live oak, a nest that will fall in the wind. I told you one morning a person is an empty train moving through the mountains at night and waking a woman who listens to the wind in the trees when the train has passed. She gets up and goes outside in her nightgown, walks across the chilly grass and steps into the creek that runs across her land. She stands there feeling the cold water and the stones, returns to her house and lies back down. Her skin is the color of a candle in the dark.

And you whom I've loved forever disagreed, asserting that a person is something else entirely, a subway car full of sweating strangers, rushing under the river at night while tugboats and tankers negotiate the currents and flounders look up from the mud. A person is the newspaper that falls to the floor, amongst all those aching subway feet, and a person is the woman who leans to pick it up, smoothes it gently and begins to read.

She will walk home soon through the balmy summer streets, to her husband who's cooking and singing as he waits for her. A person is the sidewalk that leads to her front stoop. A person is the music she hears in the distance, a song she remembers from church. She hums it, growing hungry as she walks. A person, I said then, is the glass of wine she savors, the bottle she shares with her husband. But another kind of person is the bike someone stole from the rack in front of the library, a bike which was given in love, for Christmas, that's being stripped now and spray-painted gold. On other days a person is more like the opossum with a baby in her pouch, who sniffs at the back door. We watch her push the garbage can around, trying to knock it over but afraid of hurting her baby if the can falls over on her, so she gives up and walks off across the weedy grass to look for papaya, broken open and rotting, or for mango and starfruit waiting in the bushes. A person is that appetite for sweetness in the dark.

Until it Grows too Dark

My silence is walking through a strange city in the rain, a city whose language he doesn't understand. He has no money in his pockets. His wallet holds only snapshots. My silence is walking because there's nothing else to do; he's not looking for anything particular; he's not sure where he is. His own silence, which is buried far deeper inside him, tells him to keep walking, keep looking. *Something will show itself,* his silence seems to say. This man, my silence, loves to read stories to his children, sitting in the garden in the late afternoon. Now, in this strange city, he steps into a bodega to ask for help but feels suddenly too shy to approach the stern-looking woman at the cash register or the skinny kid mopping the floor. So my silence steps back out into the rain. He keeps walking while his own silence reassures him everything will be alright. Eventually he finds a small park with benches sheltered beneath a lean-to where he can sit out of the rain. Except for a few pigeons, the park is empty. And as he sits there, he grows indistinct, until he looks more like a smudge than a man.

Back where he comes from his wife and children have gathered as usual in the garden. His wife holds the book he read from yesterday. His son is impatient: he yearns to tell his dad about this girl, his classmate, who put her head down on her desk and fell so deeply asleep no one could wake her. He wants to explain how she'd spoken in her sleep, how she'd said something to him. He whispers her name. Soon the crickets and night creatures are calling back and forth and the small family is invisible in the darkness. The mother's voice is still whispering a story of some sort, but soon she too will fall silent.

The Seed

Inside my body is another tiny me, smaller than a fingernail, shaped like I am, with my fingerprints and all my memories. But this person lives outside town, in a cottage in a field of tall grass with a small stream running through, a stream he can wade and even sit down in to cool off in when the day grows hot. The water is cold there as it runs over gravel. Sometimes deer step from the pine trees at dusk when this other me is sitting on the back porch reading in the fading light, with a cup of tea. He wanders out sometimes in the near-dark and sits by the stream to look for the first stars. His wife stays inside making tapestries and baby clothes. Sometimes she works through the night and sleeps all the next day in their wood-paneled bedroom whose window looks out on the empty road. And no one plows that road in winter, so the other me inside me must walk all the way to town.

Down in the basement the potatoes ache for someone to come down there and gather them. Up in the attic, spider webs grow thick. Everyone thinks of these people with the names of trees, thinks of them turning vivid colors in the fall. *We'll go out for a drive*, someone says to his family, *and visit the hills that are red and yellow-orange, and then we'll stop in town for cider and pie.* The man and his wife wait patiently for these visitors, though they live in that field of tall grass beside pine trees, whose colors never change much, only turning slightly darker.

The Purposeful Hum

At first I couldn't believe the news that scientists had discovered a way to ascertain why each of us was born, by pricking us slightly through the moons of our thumbs and putting that tiny specimen under a high-powered microphone that can actually detect sound that lies deeper than genetics—these scientists call it *purposeful humming*. Then they amplify this sound by a billion until they can hear its harmonics. It's somewhere in these haunting harmonies that they've been able to isolate the code, the secret, to our purpose, the role we were born to fulfill. Soon, one of these scientists says, we'll be able to prick our newborns so they won't waste time trying to "find themselves," and eventually we might even be able to prick babies in utero and design our cities, our very society, by responding to what we hear there.

There's a pattern to everything, of course, including time, so it follows that birds and butterflies might be trained to fly through time without necessarily flying through space. You see? The possibilities are as exciting as discovering another organ inside the body, a sponge-like part of ourselves that can soak up the memories we don't want anymore and squeeze them back out as newly-minted fractals of experience that make us feel so good we might almost say we're happy.

It's like the time our subway stopped beneath the river. The doors slid open and everyone got out, pulled back the curtains of darkness that hung there and walked into a place and time where they were exactly who they should have been, even if they should have been ugly or alone, which hardly ever happened, or they should have been a dog, or a bat, or a field mouse, which did in fact happen, more often than you might expect.

And then the curtain closed again, and the empty train moved forward through the dark.

The Driftwood House

I have been smaller than the days we forget, smaller than the dreams we remember just a moment, smaller than the hole from the poke of a needle that will heal you, smaller than the dust circulating in your blood.

So then the extinct birds began to fly around our heads and the halo of past time shone around us all. So then the extinct species of people and animals started calling from the deeper inside us, as everything mimicked our mother and our mother sat naked by the shore, on a seaweed-covered boulder. She let the waves dash her and swirl around her body, which looked fleshy and pale against the hairy rocks.

Our mother sang then like a seal, but she was still the woman who'd nursed us and kissed us goodnight, the woman who'd given us baths. We walked that beach holding hands and looking out for the dolphins we imagined might be swimming there; we listened for sea birds and *swoosh* of the waves reaching toward us and pulling away.

And so we collected driftwood to build our secret house, to live inside the dark bones of someone else's memory.

The Shoes

Have you heard of that country where people lived without shoes, because they believed that only bare feet sang to the ancestors buried in the ground, only bare feet caused the ground-people to sing back to them as they walked through the woods and fields? Have you heard the stories of how far they could walk, adorned in their shells and twigs and mica, these people who wore the scents of forest-breeze and dream? Once I kissed a girl whose feet looked like hooves, who dreamed of walking like anyone else, who swam underwater back and forth across the pool with flippers strapped on, and a snorkel. I remember how her mouth tasted, even after all these years. We sat by the sea wall while she told me of the barefoot tribe, and of her grandpa, who'd traveled to those woods with a duffel-bag stuffed with shoes he gave out there, to teach those people a new way to walk. That's when she'd kissed me. There were swans in the harbor. On the transistor radio she always carried with her, the Beach Boys sang "Caroline, No." *But once they put shoes on*, she told me, *those people never took them off, not even when they slept*. Then she took off her necklace—a pebble on a string—and draped it around my neck. Sometimes I pretend it's still there. *It was as though those boots had replaced their feet. Soon they were all wearing shoes, and their paths straightened out into pure destinations. And though they were still naked, they'd started to kick things, stomp around loudly, and sing pop songs in foreign languages.* She fell silent then, as we watched a group of boys throw a net out for minnows, which they pulled up with glee and spilled out onto the dock. The fish flip-flopped for a while; then they lay still. A few of the boys pierced the little fish for bait, but the others seemed content just to watch them slowly die.

The Small Animals

Every morning before the neighborhood swimming pool opened, I helped the lifeguard collect the water rats he'd caught in the mousetraps that often only stunned them. He'd grab the rat's tail and drop the rat into a brown paper lunch bag, scrunch the bag closed, and chuck the bagged rat as far out into the harbor as he could. Proud of his arm, he claimed he could throw a rat as far as the low-tide islands. He had slicked-back black hair and a cigarette behind the ear, and he thought he sang falsetto like a doo-wop star. So he screeched all afternoon up in his lifeguard chair, combing and petting his glistening hair, working on his suntan. He never swam: it messed up his pompadour. Years later I heard he'd gone off to Vietnam and that he cried now uncontrollably and punched the empty air. He was probably just a few years older than I was, but I flushed with pride when he called out my name or gave me the thumbs up when I did jackknives off the diving board. And the girls I had secret crushes on stood at the foot of his lifeguard chair, faces turned up to him like sunflowers, giggling and snapping their fingers to the radio tunes they all sang along with, the songs I practiced at night that summer, in my basement bedroom, while my parents lumbered and mumbled upstairs, turning off the lights and locking the doors. Then they called down goodnight to me, one after the other. My brother and sister were already sleeping. I could hear small animals moving through the dark, just outside my window, and I wondered what their lives were like. So I turned off my light and just lay there listening.

The Double Dream of Sleeping

One night, my wife and I dreamed the same dream: we had carried our mattress to the ocean, thrown it into the water and climbed on. We lay together in that bed as we drifted out into the deep water, in a night that was teeming with stars and silence. We slept deeply in the lulling motion of the waves, as we dreamed we were sitting in a cafe by a ski lift, drinking coffee and watching people slide down the mountain. The language we were speaking is not the one we speak, but we understood each other perfectly well. By then our mattress had drifted out of sight, and fish had started circling—but we were still sleeping, dreaming that we'd decided to ride the ski lift to the top of the mountain, despite the fact that we had no skis, that our clothes were barely warm enough for the outdoor cafe.

At some point my wife woke and looked out at the ocean's taut body, at the water which was so calm it seemed to have been oiled. She took off her nightgown and slipped off the mattress. She swam away while I dreamed I was freezing at the top of that mountain, looking out across the valley. By the time she was out of sight, I too had awakened on our mattress, alone in the ocean.

When I heard my name being called from the distance, I dove in to follow her voice.

As I swam I could see clear to the bottom, where the precious things we'd collected in all our years together were assembled as though it was a huge room we could live in. Our books and CDs and family photographs, our clothes and instruments and computers, all these things sat on the floor of the ocean, as though waiting for us to return. We pulled toward each other, hoping to wake up soon, before we felt the impulse to swim down there too, to start something else we could never turn back from, as vivid and empty as the moon.

Solitude

I came across a rack of antlers jutting from the dead-low tide line. There must be a head, I thought, still bristling with fur, with a mouth and nostrils and eyes, buried just below, and a whole body just below that. Fishing line was tangled in the antlers--the only litter I'd seen on that beach--and there were tiny feathers caught in that filament, down or dust or hummingbird wings. So I unwound that line for the feathers and took it home in a bundle that looked like a nest. I put it under my pillow and fell asleep at dusk.

Next morning a flock of small birds lay on my front stoop, with bright yellow bellies and silky wings. I hadn't heard them slam against my glass door. As I breathed across each delicate body, it stirred to life; and then it was standing, quivering, singing its one note and flying off. Soon I was throwing birds into the sky.

Overnight the tide had fallen even further. Huge fish had been stranded. They flapped and quivered as they suffocated. I headed out through the muck in my hip boots with a bucket. I poured water over their bodies and sang a song that makes the tide rise.

If that didn't work, I thought I'd start a fire and drag those fish up to the beach, gut them for a solitary feast that might last deep into the evening: Good food must not be wasted, I told myself again.

But that evening, as the tide rose, the strange deer returned, with branches on their heads, full of nests full of birds. They walked along the beach, poised like those women you've seen—but only on TV--who carry massive baskets of food on their heads, across great distances, always looking straight ahead, to keep those baskets balanced.

11

Duet

1.

Then certain of the lucky people started to assert that they were entitled to own other less lucky people's silence. Silence, they argued, was a privilege not a right, and they started to appropriate that silence, not by making *noise* exactly, but by making sure those less lucky others stayed awake for so many hours that their heads buzzed with static and gibberish. The lucky ones did this with light at first, then by drugging the air with a caffeine-like perfume, until merely breathing was like snorting speed--a great ride at first with a deep sadness to follow. Some of us still believed sadness made us real, so we breathed more deeply. It was hard enough already to earn enough money to rent sufficient darkness to cover us all night. So we all bought machines that mimicked the sounds of wind and rain, we yelled when we spoke to each other. And we tried to ignore the noise inside our heads. Most of the non-human creatures had vanished to the south, where silence was still free. And even here, life seemed in many ways unchanged. Children went off to school and play while adults spent their time as adults always have. Our families and skin were still ours; our eyes and mouths and whom we fell in love with, whom we desired and kissed, these were still ours. The sky was still blue. Fruit was still sweet. We counted our blessings, giving thanks to what we could.

2.

Because our house was infested with termites, we hired exterminators to wrap it in a tent and fill the tent with deadly fumes. That's the normal procedure in this part of the world. Deadly poison gas wafted into our closets and drawers, our books and clothing and pillows--every nook and cranny of our house--killing even the most miniscule creatures, including the mold in our bathrooms and closets, the moths in our clothes and lizards in our walls. When the tent came off, the house had to stand open for a full day before anyone could safely return. And for the first few days back inside the house, we were afraid to breathe deeply: Who knew where the gas might be lurking? Then we started smelling the dead animals that had been caught in the walls and in the crawl space beneath the house, the stray cat we'd fed for years, which we'd thought had run off somewhere. There he lay in the semi-dark beneath our living room floor, swollen and stinking and covered in flies. So we duct-taped a rake to the end of a pole; we reached in to roll him and shovel him out. We buried him beneath the banana trees, heavy with bunches of finger-sized fruits we hardly ever noticed until they'd turned soft and were eaten with gusto by the squirrels and the wasps.

Bones

There are full tides and secret tides, slack tides and whirlpools, whether you live near the ocean or not. There are beaches like shelves that stretch so far out into the ocean we might walk to the horizon only up to our knees and then jump off, far out there, into a bottomless wilderness, a forest of tree-sized seaweed full of its own stars and a sweeping undercurrent powerful enough to strip your clothes off and carry you to places you thought you'd only know about by reading. As though the breaking waves carried skeletons, rib cages and backbones and threw them at our feet as we walked along talking of the newest kinds of wind, created by the satellites we'd thought would simply float above us, allowing us to talk on our phones. But now we know our own inventions have shifted the breezes and the minerals in our blood, where certain of our most ancient thoughts live, as though the mastodons in there were waking to set out across a landscape of melting snow, looking for whatever food they ate when they actually lived, eons ago. *If you taste the water, the pretty lifeguard told us, you'll notice it's faintly soapy. This is for your protection,* she said; *that soap taste is actually dust-motes of pulverized bones from the healthiest children we've found in the various day-care centers set up across the city. Don't worry: No children were hurt in the process; in fact they felt a great relief. We only used the extra bones.*

II.

The Night-Blooming Cactus

One afternoon, my son and I climbed the huge avocado tree that grew in our back yard. There were small pools in the crotches where branches met the trunk, and in each grotto-pool there were tiny water lilies. Matt found a little toad—only about the size of a fingernail--who leapt from that branch into the grass below. We sat there and thought about that leap. Then we sat a while longer in the shade, hardly talking, watching the world as though we might glimpse some sort of secret. There were cactus plants above us, hanging down through the near-darkness.

Sometimes, when the moon grew full, those cactus plants blossomed, calling the night-bees and the moths into that canopy. We never climbed up to smell those darkness-flowers. By morning they'd withered and dropped their petals to the grass.

The Houses

So many families have started living in our trees: when we walk through our neighborhood in the evenings, we hear whispering above our heads, and the rustling of bodies that aren't owls, or squirrels. The houses that were once so well-maintained are empty now, their lawns unkempt, their mailboxes overflowing with fliers and magazines, their windows broken. Who knew such solid dreams could fall so quickly to ruin? The packs of stray dogs are mostly harmless, though they make messes no one cleans up, so we shoo them from our yard, whose two trees hold families we've gotten to know, at least a little, since the adjustment began. We sometimes bring them food, and they watch things for us, when we have to go out for some reason. It's strange to still be living in a house, after almost everyone else has moved into the trees, but it holds all our books and musical instruments, and where would we—*who* would we—be without those precious things? I know I'm no musician, but still I love to play. I sit at night, even now, strumming my guitar, while my family and the tree-families sing along with me.

Since the humans have taken over the trees and the meadows and the woods, the birds we love have had nowhere to live, so we've transformed our rooms into wild places for them, we've opened our windows to let them fly in, fly home as it were, since we've made these places real—or real enough, it seems, to convince these lovely creatures. Often now, in the afternoon, I sit playing my guitar while the people outside in the sunny summer trees debate questions like which of the candidates might restore their savings and their televisions, which candidate might figure out how to keep the wind out of their trees.

Inside our bird-filled house, the woods and fields stretch farther each day, in response to those birds and our singing. There will be migrations, this year, for the first time, inside a house. And soon enough the forest will stretch so many miles, our children will be able to venture out with only their gumption and start a new life there, for themselves and their families, all in this house we've refused to leave. And maybe, if what we are doing here is noticed, other families will move back into their old homes, restore the rooms and animals like we have, until slowly each house will become itself again, alive and aching with its ancient mysteries of fur, and pollen, and dust.

Living Without Names

...a model of order, even if set
in a place which is full of doubt...
                    --Ian Hamilton Finlay

1.

A stone dropped into the ocean may fall for weeks before it touches bottom. Most of that fall is through absolute darkness. As it falls, the weight of the ocean presses in. It seems to move more slowly as it sinks deeper. It drifts, as it falls, with the ocean's secret currents. It is just a stone, but someone dropped it there.

2.

She lives in a city without a name, in a country no one remembers anymore. The streets are already crowded with pedestrians when she steps out each morning to hurry off to work. She moves anonymously through the crowds, reluctant to be recognized. But in fact all the faces in this city are the same, and in fact no one looks at each other as they walk.

Her job is to put the white back into milk. Other people deal with snow, still others with skin, and eggs, and eyes.

Out in the country in this country no one knows, wild animals build houses and tend to the farms. No one here speaks badly of wolves, and foxes are admired for their wit and style. The bears in their caves are thought of as philosophers.

And when the bombs fall, everyone dances. These dances resemble old full-moon harvest hoedowns, even as the dancers are blown to smithereens.

3.

Since her parents had grounded her and she hated watching TV, she lay on her bed and wondered if she could fit a river into her body, if the river were the size of her veins or the nerves that branched out everywhere. And if so, what would the source of that river be? And would that river join other rivers, growing larger every few miles, until it reached the sea? Maybe it was more like a mountain stream, with waterfalls whose water was so clean she could drink it, so refreshing when she swam there she felt clean through and through, and happier, almost, than it was possible to be. And what about the landscape that river flowed through? Would it be possible to fit it in her, too?

4.

Then I remembered a story about sleeping outside in the rain, lying on my back in the middle of a field while horses grazed nearby. My wife sat next to me, singing softly in the rain, which felt cool and refreshing after weeks of parched silence. At some point I woke and started singing her song, as though her voice had handed it over to mine, like a plate of delicious and nourishing food. As I sang, she fell silent, lay down and fell asleep. The horses drew closer. The rain stopped then, like an unfinished sentence, and the sudden silence roused her. We stood up together and walked toward the trees, which seemed to back away as we stepped closer. Behind us, the horses collapsed into the grass, and a smell of horse sweat filled the air...

5.

Behind every face is another, with slightly different wrinkles and a different slant of nose, but essentially the same as the one that meets the world. And beneath that face is another just about the same. Sometimes you can glimpse the movement of these under-faces as they scowl or laugh at what the surface is saying.

In that way we're like fish moving just beneath the surface of a lake, making faint ripples no one can see from shore, while a breeze blows an empty rowboat slowly to the other side, toward the dark trees that lean there watching their own reflections in the dark water and shaking themselves sometimes—you've seen them—like dancers shaking their bodies loose before they begin the performance.

The Ordinary Wonders

Taking out the compost after days of rain, I almost walk through the freshly-woven spider web stretched between two palm trees. So I kneel there watching, to see what that spider's up to. There's a female cardinal in the still-dripping fire-cracker bush that stretches out above my head, and I wonder if she might be the same little bird who flapped against my study window a few hours ago, then tumble-wrestled with another bird before flying off. I'm watching the spider web but nothing's happening, so I blow softly across it, meaning no harm, and out scampers the spider from behind a shriveled leaf, into the center of his web. Is he looking up at me? I stop blowing. Clouds are moving quickly across the sky. I can feel them as I stand here watching my spider, who watches his human. And now a real breeze awakens in the trees, quivering the web. Unlike my breath, the breeze doesn't seem to alarm the little spider in the least. He walks now, *strolls* we might even say, back to his shriveled leaf and slips under. And as I lean down to pick up the bowl of scraps I hear my neighbor singing next door, a full-throated jingle of lust and abandon. So I hold myself still, just to listen.

Windows, Mirrors, Chandeliers

Yesterday, riding our bikes in the Everglades, my wife and I noticed a large group of vultures about 100 yards ahead, hopping around a carcass. A man with a camera stood amongst them, but they seemed to pay him no attention. As we approached the group we could see that the birds were tearing the last bits of flesh from the skeleton of a huge alligator, the bones of whose tail lay scattered across the narrow road. The photographer smiled quietly as we passed, so still that the vultures had forgotten he was there. They started landing again as soon as we'd passed. Of course I thought of Tibetan sky burials, the sacred vultures that so thoroughly clean the human carcasses set out for them that the bones are scoured, denuded of the ichors of flesh. How high do those sacred birds fly, shitting their human remains across the land?

Somewhere, I've heard, they've developed a way of cremating the body and mixing a small amount of the beloved's ash into panes of glass, so those who still live will be able to look *through* their beloved, through glass that is only slightly foggy with the eternally-preserved fragments of bone and sinew, those precious remains. Might a whole house be equipped with windows tinted with loved ones' ashes, stained glass windows of a sort, grayish or flecked with fur-like particles? The kitchen windows might be cloudy with father's dust, while ashy smudges of mother's dark hair might dye the bedroom dormers. We could look through our loved ones as we looked out at the world. So every house we lived in might feel like church again, and looking out through our windows might become a form of prayer.

The Gleaming

She was living alone that summer, in a cabin nestled in the trees beside a small lake she swam in each morning, before anyone else was around, sometimes even before sunrise.

She loved the smell of the water before the sun warmed it, and she loved the way she felt as she climbed out, to shiver in the tall grass for a moment before starting to dry her body. Then she ran up the small rise to the cabin, to the camping stove she kept on the picnic table outside; she made herself a cup of tea and sat in her camp chair as she watched the day grow full.

She swam every morning of that summer, and even into autumn, when the grass was crisp with hints of frost and the wind drew sharp ruffles across the surface of the lake. She swam even in heavy rain, singing while she swam, since her voice stayed so close to her body in the rain. She spent her days drawing or walking or reading. She rarely spoke more than a few words aloud.

In the evenings she made a simple dinner. Then she sat by the lake's edge with a glass of wine and watched the bats swoop and zigzag, and watched the fireflies flicker in the grass.

One evening, five deer stepped from the trees and walked down to the lake where she sat. They walked so close she could smell them; then they stepped into the lake, one after the other, and drank. They slurped loudly at the water—she was surprised at this—then turned as one body, like a school of fish, and walked back into the trees. She thought for a moment she might follow them.

During those last weeks of autumn, a man came to visit her. The cabin filled with voices. They held hands as they walked around the lake in the evening. They made roaring fires. She continued to swim every morning, and sometimes he joined her. She always wore a bathing suit after he arrived. He'd swim across the whole lake and walk back through the grass. Sometimes, she'd walk through that tall grass to meet him. Her teeth chattered as she walked, but her eyes were always gleaming.

Ode

1.

My brother would get lost, sometimes, walking home. He'd take the wrong bus or walk the wrong direction, singing to himself so he wouldn't get scared, speaking another little boy's name when people leaned over to ask if they could help. Sometimes he'd climb a tree or swim out to the crop of low-tide rocks we called an island, and sometimes he'd make a clubhouse in the woods and hide there. He liked to ride escalators up and down, and he loved to pretend he was a mannequin.

One day he hid himself inside his best friend, who was headed to the movies with his parents. He and his friend sat together as though they were one little boy, eating buttered popcorn, covering their eyes when the monster in the film chased the family through the woods. And my brother saw us, his family, up there on the screen, he saw the monster grab our sister as though he would eat her--and he grew too scared to stay there. So he left that theatre by himself while no one was looking; he walked out into the evening and the quickly-falling snow.

2.

Both my brother and I carried rabbit's feet with us in those days, attached by a small chain to a belt loop. His was dyed bright red; mine a dull grey. They kept us lucky.

And then there were the rabbit fur winter gloves, so soft and warm. They smelled like living animals, as though they were our pets. I loved to hold them up to my nose and breathe. Our hands smelled like fur when we took those gloves off, as though they were a different kind of animal than we were, attached to us but somehow also wild.

We never ate rabbit stew or roasted rabbit or any rabbit at all.

We did own pet rabbits for a while, two white ones with pale eyes and bright pink veins sketched along their ears. Their fur was as soft as the insides of our gloves. My brother and mother loved them. My sister and father and I ignored them—as well as we could. They lived in a wood-and-wire hutch in the back yard, and sometimes my mother would let them out to run around in the grass.

The lives of those pet rabbits ended sadly when my mother caught a wild rabbit who'd come into the yard. It was tawny and skinny, with shorter ears than our pets, but since it seemed mild-mannered—had it been a pet too?--she thought she should keep it. So she put it in the hutch with the others.

We didn't hear a thing, but next time we looked in, the two pet bunnies had been slashed to death by the wild one. They lay in bloody pieces scattered across the wire mesh floor. So my mother opened the hutch door and the wild rabbit leaped out and dashed away. She hosed out the hutch and gave it to some neighbors.

We also had gerbils, horned toads, and frogs; finches that suffocated one morning when our father burned breakfast; turtles of all sorts; a fish tank full of fish that ate each other's tails off; and a boa constrictor.

Mostly we forgot they were there, except to feed them.

That Stranger's Continent

I wonder how many microscopic creatures live inside my body, eating other tiny creatures in there, creating other little creatures, making waste and growing hungry. I've heard that there are whole nations of such creatures in every organ and orifice, and I've heard that these creatures are specific to me, or to you—that is, since they've evolved with us they can live only in us; they think and dream and move and sing specifically as creatures within us. I'd bet there are more creatures inside each of us than there are people in the world. Imagine finding yourself somehow amongst that crowd, inside your own body, shrunk to their size. Would you feel hopelessly lost, or might you recognize someone from your past? Might you call out to him in your new language? And might he turn to you then with a squint and a shrug and suddenly break out smiling?

When I lived in the city, I'd occasionally bump into someone I'd almost totally forgotten. Wending through the midtown crowds during rush hour, some man or woman about my age would knock into me as though purposefully, step back and yelp a name. Sometimes that name was mine, in which case I'd suddenly remember him or her and we'd stand there talking while the crowds rushed past. We'd exchange phone numbers then, kiss or shake hands fondly and step back into the fray.

One evening, I bumped into a woman I'd played hide-and-seek with, once, maybe twice, when our parents had a barbeque. I'd hid in the bushes with her. She'd held my hand. I don't remember if we were ever caught or if we made it home free. I do know that as I spoke to her, twenty-five years later, I remembered her smell, like suntan lotion, that had lingered on my own hand after hers had pulled away. Here she was standing in the street in the city-dusk, talking about her husband and children, her full and perfectly ordinary life. When we kissed chastely in parting, we must have shared at least a few microscopic creatures that had been only ours, until we kissed. Maybe some small number of our tiniest selves survived, in that foreign country, that stranger's continent, and are hiding in the darkness of that hide-and-seek still, breathing each other's sweet blossoming, hoping no one will find them.

The Animals

The mouse inside my guts is just a mouse, and an ordinary one at that. I could say I love him, despite myself, for his sleek fur and the way he sniffs at the seeds and secrets deep in there, where I don't even realize I've hidden them, which will grow now into sunflowers or flowering bushes inside me, since by nudging and chewing he's dislodged them from their dormancy. The sunflowers may even grow larger than my body, which scares me a bit, to be honest. And they'll attract bees and small birds, and they'll sway in the sun until, nodding, they'll drop whatever is left of their seeds. And what kinds of birds are they, after all, that eat those seeds? How far do they migrate; what songs do they sing?

When I was a child we owned a boa constrictor that needed to be fed only once a month. He ate rats and mice my mother collected from the cancer research institute downtown. These rodents had been shot full of toxic chemicals, cut open and sewed up like the patched jeans we wore then, and most of them could barely walk. My mom would place them gently in the terrarium, where they'd stand shaking or tottering aimlessly around—until the snake got them into his mouth. Still alive when he swallowed them, their tails moved like conductor's batons beating spastic time to a music we couldn't hear, until they were just a lump in that silky-rope body.

I never took much pleasure in that snake, or in watching the rats disappear there—or in any of the other exotic pets my mother collected, tortoises which moved so rarely we only knew they'd died when we smelled them rotting, piranhas which banged against their tanks when we walked by, yearning to take a nice bite of our faces. I wasn't even that fond of *dogs* in those days—they seemed always to get hit by cars or to disappear into the neighborhood somewhere, and my parents would ask me to go out on my bike and search for them in the chilly dusk. I'd ride up and down the streets calling "Tippy!" calling "Otis!" without luck. And when I returned we'd have dinner, by candlelight, while the hamsters in the kitchen ran on their wheels, which made a halfhearted creaking music, like an old door being opened and closed, over and over, to let nothing in or out.

The Tiny Grandma

I woke up covered in baby powder, sneezing and wondering why the air conditioner was turned down nearly to freezing. The tile floor around my bed was dusted in powder, with traces of footsteps left by a barefoot person with delicate feet, and a large-pawed dog. I was naked; my body felt taut and well-rested. Even with the air-conditioner churning loudly, I could hear crows and blue jays calling out in annoyance, just outside the window. When I got up, I noticed I was taller than I'd been before: I almost hit the doorframe with my forehead as I left the cold room and walked into the main house, calling out to whoever might be home. In the living room, feathers covered the furniture, from burst pillows that lay limply on the floor. The whirring ceiling fan blew those feathers here and there like fake dancing snow in a Christmas window display. A radio played softly inside one of the closets; I could hear a familiar voice conducting an interview with a man who kept interrupting himself mid-sentence to sing out in a fake-operatic baritone. In the kitchen there were apples and cheese on the counter, a half-empty bottle of white wine, still cold, and out on the screen porch a huge spider web stretched across a figure in a chair. She was wearing a bathing suit, smiling up at me. The tips of her fingers were smoking like incense-scented cigarettes and her belly button glistened with a jewel. Out on the lawn, children ran back and forth through the sprinkler, laughing like we had done as kids. The air was potent with the smell of grilling hamburgers and just-cut grass. Dandelion seeds blew here and there, like fine white hair of some tiny grandma—a woman the size of a mouse or a squirrel. They flew up in the breeze as the children stopped laughing and watched me walk out there to join them.

III.

To Sing the World

Whenever I travel, the birds tell me first I'm in new country.
--Gary Young

1.

Some mornings when I step outside to fetch the paper, the darkness feels laden with the damp scents of the night as the night itself seeps into the ground. Every once in a while I startle an opossum and sometimes a whole possum family as they sniff through the bushes, heading home—wherever home is—to sleep. I imagine them sleeping as a single ball of gray fur, and I wonder what they smell like, sleeping there, underneath my house maybe, or behind some familiar bushes. I wonder how their breath sounds as they sleep. Often lately I wake in the middle of the night, startled by my own breathing, or by a dream. I lie there and listen to the hum my wife's sleeping body makes, and I listen to the clicks and shifts inside the darkness. Sometimes I grow frightened, lying there, and sometimes I realize I have wasted my life. Not all of it, of course, but a substantial sum. Certain birds fly only at night, small migrating songbirds that feel safe in the darkness. They land at first dawn in the quivering trees and sing out their adventures to each other and the world.

2.

Someone is singing from inside a house along our street, but I can't determine which house her voice is coming from. She sings beautifully, but more than beauty, her voice conveys an urgency not of pain or pleasure but of something more deeply haunting, as though someone could sing inside a tree or a stone. Or inside a bird, for that matter, inside a bird's bones, inside a bird's bones as that bird flies south, inside a bird's bones as that bird lands and sings. I walk up and down the street leaning toward each house, stilling my breath, listening, as the evening settles around us. As usual, there's no one else in the street; as usual, the houses are closed up around their secrets, as though the lives inside them were fleshless but yearning, like pollen on the breeze of a summer's afternoon.

3.

Our own house is surrounded by trees and bushes, each of which is filled with small vivid lives that are aware of us as we might be aware of many futures, potential but unformed. They don't know what we are, but they hear us moving back and forth, yelling out and lumbering across the grass. They flicker into hiding when we come too close. Eventually they may learn to ignore us. Everything we do must seem oblivious to them, the lizards and ants, spiders and snakes, all of whom have to live by their wits and are granted no second chances. Those small birds too, those butterflies and bees. When we watch them I think they must feel an unnerving pull, as though they were drowning but still able to breathe, or as though a strange energy were rearranging everything just a little, including the air.

4.

Once as a child I walked through a field of tall grass to a row of dark trees whose air was so cool it frightened me a little. The mushrooms looked like the bones of someone who wasn't completely decomposed, and the house I'd walked from looked hazy in the distance, as if it were floating slightly off the ground. So I picked up a twig and kissed it to give it magic, then hid it beneath a loaf-sized stone and started back to the house. And as I walked back, I saw my father and grandfather, smoking pipes, walking toward me through the grass. They were talking, both of them, with their teeth firmly clamped on their pipes, so their voices sounded muffled and annoyed. But they weren't annoyed at all! They'd found a turtle in the front garden and they wanted to show me. So I held their hands and we walked back together through that tall grass that was buzzing now with dragonflies and hummingbirds. I loved the smell of their pipe smoke. My grandfather smelled of hair-oil and leather, which I loved too. My brother was napping in that big house, alone in the bed we shared, surrounded by feathers we'd collected every morning before the dew had dried. My mother was reading on the shady back porch, reading and crying until she'd disappeared, while her mother—my grandma—snapped bones for the broth we would sip so discreetly after cocktails in the den. There were crows in the attic, like old photograph albums, singing their darkness, an ancient tapestry. Since the windows were open, they could fly out when they needed to, pulling the night-world behind them.

5.

I've heard this: In every cell there's something like a universe, energies and relationships that function like our stars and planets, like our light and lives. And these cells, in relationship, are the only world we can truly know. But what about the universe inside each of these cells? Could we somehow, someday, slip in there and live, for one tiny moment, as a moment in that universe? What would we see there? And what about those cells inside the cells inside us? Are they virtual universes too? What's time there? What's distance? What's love? Inside our bodies, in the secret places, there are large-shouldered animals moving slowly through the tall grass, watched over by wolves whose breath can be seen as the dusk-air grows cool. There has never been a human there, but somehow we can listen to the shuffle of these huge beasts' legs as they move, and we can hear their hooves step lightly. That's how many of them there are, right now inside us, moving across the landscape. Each heartbeat in each of their bodies beats inside us, deeper than anyone has ever ventured, or ever will.

6.

I'm out of fire, someone says to the trees, *and I'm almost out of air*. I see him standing there on the sidewalk, hear him from my lawn chair nestled almost in the bushes. Now he leans and picks up a pebble, marble-shoots it straight up in the air and stands there watching it rise and fall, a man about my age, who hasn't noticed me. Then he mutters, *oh the hell with it*, and walks quickly on, as though going somewhere in a hurry. I am reading Jack Gilbert, who died a few months ago, listening carefully to his language-carvings in the still air, wondering at the urgency of everything he said, at the seed-urgent pull of his need for primal love, the love that makes us cry in our fingerprints and teeth, for the taste of the mica in the stone. I know so few of the creatures all around me, buzzing and humming and yearning to eat me, going about their supremely healthy lives. I am only what I am now, fragments of the larger breath. And no one else passes on the sidewalk for hours, and no one else drives down the street, though many birds continue to fly overhead, some so high all I can see of them is blue.

7.

And if I took the same walk every day for a year, what would I see there and who would I be? There is evidence of broken bones, broken bottles, broken wings. Everywhere we look there are reasons to go home. If I took the same walk every day for a decade, one phase of my life to another, would I learn something valuable about memory and pain? I am almost myself almost all of the time, almost never completely. But what does that mean to the mouse in my study, behind the chair I read in, and what does that matter to the wind through the trees, which ruffles the fur on the squirrel who chatters at the shadows moving across the lawn? The grass in another world grows without stopping, grows deeper and deeper until each blade is like a tree, and the forest is tight and flimsy and green, and the light that shines through it feels hollow, like a bone. Mind is a dream, like the moon in the trees when the trees shift and sway, just a little, in the breeze. Is there anything anywhere that lives without mind? Is that snail not singing as he glides across the sidewalk into the fresh-cut, dewy evening grass?

Satellites

You love rowing out across the lake when the sun is just lighting the sky to the east, behind the soft mountains you've never explored. There's a thermos of coffee lying in the gunwale, wrapped in an old tee shirt. Sometimes there's a book on the bench beside you, though this early in the morning it's too dark to read. Your wife is awake too, on shore, looking out toward you occasionally as she sits with her sketch pad and tea. She, too, is waiting for the light. The lake is still; a slight mist rises. Sometimes a school of fish ripples the water; sometimes a solitary bird flies overhead, so close you can see its white belly against the lightening sky. You row steadily for half an hour; then you let yourself drift while you open your thermos and drink. You think of old friends, old loves, of the people you didn't love enough when they needed you. Sometimes as the day lights, you watch the distant shore through binoculars; you watch your wife sitting in the first light, looking out across the lake to where she thinks you must be drifting. She can't be sure, since you're out beyond her sight. It's chilly for swimming, but you do so anyway, naked—like a secret. Sometimes, after a swim, you just sit in that small boat, shivering and drinking coffee, naked and grieving and joyous at your life, at all the life around you, all the life that doesn't know you as anything other than some *thing* in the world, something real and solid as a boat. Then you stand up and, balancing carefully, naked, you wave to your wife—just a speck on the shore—and she seems to wave back. So you let yourself drift even further out. You lean back on a cushion, look up at the sky, and imagine the satellites hidden in the blue, watching you, understanding nothing.

No Such Thing

As a child I learned how to hold burning candles in my fists without snuffing the flame or burning my hands, though I never wore gloves. My father was impressed. He'd always insisted I was talented in ways I didn't give myself credit for: feeding the dog at just the right moment or keeping the morning newspaper clean when I slipped it from its plastic sheath. He raised my allowance when I held out my glowing fists one evening after I'd kissed him goodnight, and he recited "The Hollow Men," his favorite poem, to celebrate. Then he thanked the good lord my headpiece wasn't filled with straw. Neither was his, though he did love to stuff dried leaves down his shirt for the itch they gave him, an itch that was *good for the soul* he insisted as he reminded my mother how to bark like a beagle, not like the little toy bulldog she fancied, and explained to my sister how to take an all-day bath. He was always reminding us to make sure our flashlights were filled with fresh batteries and to check our water bottles for particles of food, as potentially dangerous as too much sleep. And when I tried putting a candle in my mouth, when I managed to keep it burning in there, he knew I was destined to become as renowned as the old man upstairs, who made spider webs from dust he collected from the corners and wove into webs like hammocks he claimed we could sleep in. Since it was difficult to talk with that candle stuck in my head, I only nodded and smiled. My brother was showing how well he could sleep and watch TV at the same time, and the pet hamster was racing around his squeaky wheel while my dad practiced singing in his operatic tenor about the magic inherent in science and pain. Soon we were singing along with him, all of us, in voices that guttered and croaked like frogs--or like humans whose minds held no words at all. And then we just sat there, like silence.

Sand

He learned to walk so that every step he took made him less substantial, more nearly transparent. Sometimes, strolling with his wife in the evening, he paled into a ghost; and when he walked to the grocery store he was often invisible as air by the time he arrived. Then he could gather his groceries without paying, since his touch also made things invisible. And what else could he do? He lay down invisible each night and grew slowly opaque toward morning. When he slept late some weekends he woke clogged by the weight of his sleeping, and he had to walk in place for a while before he could get dressed. He dreamed he might become a breeze someday by taking a long hike in the mountains he loved, so he'd blow off into places he couldn't have anticipated, staying awake the whole time.

One summer morning at the beach with his family, he found himself melting into the water. He called to his wife as a wave broke through him and she waded out and gathered him up in a bucket. Then she poured him out along the sand. Slowly she gathered and patted the sand until he found himself again, a body burning pink, full of tides and brine and made out of sand now, each grain of which had once been a boulder. He loved the way she patted and molded his body, the seaweed she gathered and draped across his nakedness. He loved the way she sang softly as she worked, as though she were singing only to him, and he tried to sing along with her. But he could only whisper.

The Hurricane

Last night while we slept, someone stole all our windows. They unscrewed the frames and pulled the glass from the wall, made our house into a cave with many awkward entrances. I woke this morning to the cooing of mourning doves in our bedroom, the patter of rain on the expensive wood floors. So I got up and wandered through the house in a daze, examining our garden through the empty window frames. I leaned my head outside and let the rain drench me.

Then I threw a book out there, through the empty picture window, into the sodden grass. It was a book I'd disliked for a long time, a classic, and it felt good to see it splayed out there in the rain. I searched through my bookshelves for other books I detested. Then I went around, still undressed, pitching other objects out through this window or that: knickknacks and junk mail, cheap vases, old shoes. I stood as far back from each window as possible and threw hard, like the pitcher I once imagined I could be.

When my clamor woke the children, they helped me scatter bird seed on the furniture and carpets. We made bird baths from the cups and cereal bowls, grottoes for nests where the books had lived, lined up alphabetically for easy reference--as though the life I'd imagined I had built could be organized by author and made to cohere. We waited for a long time before we woke my wife, who smiled in her dreams and rolled over to embrace the pillow I'd slept on. She muttered snippets and coos: small birds flying through the rain, the tiny cries they sing out to each other as they fly.

A breeze was moving briskly through the house by then, and all sorts of brightly-colored birds were arriving. My wife wasn't up yet but I knew she'd be pleased to see them gathered there, singing, making nests. I knew she'd be happy we'd scattered that seed, pleased with the way we'd transformed our house from disaster to refuge while she'd been sleeping. The breeze smelled like night-blooming jasmine and orange blossoms, fragrances that make us feel happy and alive. I sat there watching birds roost in my living room, listening to my children as they walked through the garden, cooing and gathering the junk I'd thrown out there, crying out now and then at their useless broken toys.

40

The Other Woman

Walking home through the early dark, carrying yellow flowers for his wife, he passed a car parked half on the sidewalk and half in the street. As he walked around it he could see that it was filled with moths, which beat gently against the windows, as though they could slip through and fly up to the streetlight. The street was quiet. He cupped his free hand against the driver's side window and looked in: the car was otherwise empty. He looked around: all the buildings lining the street were dark, and though the sky still held faint light, it would soon be fully dark as well. He tried the car's door and was surprised to find it open. Surely those moths would want to fly free. What should he do? He thought of his wife and the flowers he'd bought her, that would make her so happy, at least for a moment. He set them down on the pavement and slipped into the car, waving his hands to shoo the moths free. He would do this for a few minutes, then get out and walk home with his flowers. Maybe she was cooking something special for him, right now, or maybe she'd opened a fresh bottle of wine. She'd love the fact that he'd thought of her, that he'd gotten just the kind of flowers she loved most. But instead of flying free, the moths had started landing on his face, in his hair. They stuck themselves to him so tightly he couldn't wave them loose; when he brushed at them more violently their guts smeared all over his hair and shirt. What a mistake! Just a minute ago he'd been smartly groomed; now he was covered in moth-gunk and wing-dust. So he stepped out of the car and picked up his flowers, which were only slightly worse for the wear. He slammed the car door and turned to walk home with some of those moths still clinging to him, as the car's alarm let forth a huge siren, which echoed up and down the street, causing other car alarms to wail loudly in response. And the moths beat against him as though he were a street light even as he started running, chased now by a beautiful woman he hadn't noticed before, who swung a butterfly net around her head and cried "Stop! It's hopeless! You'll never get away!"

Ghosts

1.

So maybe our scientists can make things in the lab to mitigate the effects of global warming and other ills that define our time, though I somehow doubt it, at least when we're talking about miniscule creatures that eat oil spill pollution and fart out fresh air, or little beings smaller than a snippet of time that can somehow supply power for the whole United States. And we're not talking atoms here. We're talking new ideas about what makes creature-life itself. I hear there are ghosts now that can do all those things no one would ever do with a real body. These synthetic lives don't need food or love, and they never sleep. They just fade away at some point that's been pre-determined in the lab.

2.

Once when I was swimming by myself in the bay, a school of mullet surrounded me and swam along with me. Each was about the length of my arm. The fish broke the surface of the water with their backs as they swam, and they nudged me sometimes with their snouts. Our bodies together made a ghostlike presence on the floor of the bay as we swam. The fish seemed curious about me, as though I was a long-lost ancestor, and they hardly flinched when I reached out to touch them.

As I swam I wondered vaguely what poisons lived in the bay: oil from our vehicles, dispersants from our spills, lawn chemicals to keep our front yards green. What was I swimming through? Why was I alone? When I reached shore, I stepped out and watched the mullet bunch up in the shallows for a moment as though waiting for me to slide back in. Then, like one body, they turned and swam away.

The Guest

My neighbor and I are standing out in the front yard talking about hurricanes and climate change, when a large white bird comes walking down our street. It has a plastic grocery bag draped around its neck.

We stop talking, hoping to make ourselves invisible, but my neighbor has a cold and can't help sneezing. Amazingly, the white bird starts sneezing in response.

As long as my neighbor keeps sneezing, the bird stands still. So I walk over and reach out to slip the plastic bag from around its neck. The bird shivers and tries to fly away. But it has only one wing, so it just leaps up, twirls around a few times, and smacks itself face first, flat in the street. It lies there without moving.

Now my neighbor coughs while I approach the sprawled body, as large as a child, and lean down to stroke its feathers, to see how badly it is injured. I've hardly touched it when its other wing comes off in my hands, just snaps off as though it were a kind of replaceable part. It's as light as a balsa-wood model airplane. I lay it gently down beside my bird, whose long neck is so gracefully curved I want to keep stroking it.

I yearn to sing to this bird. My neighbor is gagging now behind me as I lift the white body in my arms and carry it into the house to lay it on the bed in our son's childhood bedroom, wondering what a bird like this eats, hoping my neighbor will move the broken wing from the street so it won't get crushed by traffic.

I'm already thinking of names I could give it, this bird that is waking now, watching me intently out of its flat black, inexpressive eyes. I don't even know what kind of bird it is, or where it might have come from. I pull the covers up over its quivering body; I lean down to kiss it gently, whispering *sleep tight*.

IV.

The Teacher

One evening, walking alone beside the town park, the teacher noticed a group of wildflowers she hadn't seen the day before. She leaned to breathe them, and then she picked a few flowers, feeling guilty as she did so, and slipped them into her blouse, between her breasts. As she walked, their perfume mixed with her own, which produced an even more potent fragrance.

By the time she got home, the flowers were too wilted to save in water, and their scent had faded. So she went back out and picked more flowers, which she hid in different places beside her body.

And she kept walking back and forth through most of the night, until she'd picked all the wildflowers. Her whole body smelled of flowers now.

The next day she took a walk at her lunch break, looking for flowers, and came back holding a bouquet. She handed a flower to each of her students, asking them please to smell deeply. They all chattered happily at this welcome diversion.

Then the school day was over and she was still alone, surrounded by the flowers her students had discarded when the bell had released them.

In the world my father remembered, his teacher walked home then, looking for wilder, more fragrant flowers, afraid she might touch a flower that would burn her hand yet yearning to touch one that would burn her to the core. And by the time she reached home she was covered with bees gathering pollen from her flower-fragrant body.

And everyone assumed she'd found her happiness at last.

The Mushrooms

Perhaps the best way to live beyond our human span is to become a mushroom in the woods, to push gently through leaf-rot and damp soil and stand there for a few days, then pull back into the darkness, where the moon feels like a blanket and the rivers below you keep running in their night-world so pure it might seem they're not actually there. Your nerve-roots will spread then for many acres, reaching down below the rivulets and tree roots and empty spaces that are full of never-breathed air, and you'll come up again, next year perhaps, to taste another moon. The wind across the bay that sweeps into your face now is full of tiny flecks of skin and dandruff, and it smells like seaweed. The pelicans leap from their breeze-cliffs in the sky and you wish you could live in another person's mind for an hour or a day since only then might you credit yourself with whatever you already know. There are doors marked "door" and doors that look like air. We emptied our whole house onto the front lawn and sold off our possessions, everything, including our snapshots and diaries. Then we walked around the empty house naked for a while, until we were able to move away to this place, where we live in other names, displaying different talents. My past is not the past, but still it holds the truth: My mother played the violin in her upstairs apartment until she was heard by the deaf man next door, who put on his soft gloves to touch her. They sang in languages they couldn't understand and sailed around the world while I listened and learned how to dance without moving. Just as you knocked, my darling, on the back door, with a basket of mushrooms and a story of foxes and a small stream so cold it could change a person into light. The mushrooms were poison you said as you held one up and passed it to me, but we could safely slip them under our pillows, to dream on the cusp of forever.

The Homemade Pond

You thought of my wound as merely a hole I had dug in the garden for a tree I never planted. So you deepened and shaped that hole; then you filled it with water to make a small pond. You planted lily pads and papyrus, and you placed a stone in the middle of my wound—a miniature mountain—so you might sit in contemplation there. You bought a few goldfish and a solar-powered pump. You told me you loved me. You fashioned a bench, and you trimmed the bushes around my wound until they contorted like bonsai. You sat out there before dawn sometimes. Afternoons you drank a cup of tea on the bench beside me, and sometimes in the evening you brought out a beaker of sake, and you whispered to me as night fell around us.

Now, sometimes, when you're not looking, herons and snowy egrets land beside my wound. They stand so still I almost forget they're there—until all my goldfish have been snatched and swallowed. Then those huge birds fly away, *to the world beyond the mountains* the ancient poems might say, though there are no hills here, not for hundreds of miles. You'll come back tomorrow to find my fish have vanished, but you'll never notice the bird-tracks in the mud around my wound, the downy feathers in the grass.

Sometimes, throbbing while I reflect the evening sky, I can hear you inside the house blasting music on your stereo or singing songs we once sang together. And when you fall asleep, my wound picks up your dreams, as though it were a satellite dish tuned to the inner life. And sometimes while you're sleeping deeply, some sort of delicate, wild creature approaches and drinks for a long time, until it is refreshed. I can't say what kind of animal it is. Its lips feel sweet on my wound, like love.

The Grace of Our Good Luck

I arrived at my own house and knocked on the door. The person who answered was dressed just like I was. He stepped back and gestured me in. Everything was the same as I'd left it that morning: The newspaper was scattered across the dining room table, the coffee cups my wife and I had drunk from were still there, next to some crumb-dusted plates. Usually I would tidy things up, then decide what to cook for dinner. Today though was different since I was visiting myself. And neither of us spoke: no words were needed. When I smiled, he smiled back, exactly as I'd done, and when I walked through the house he did too, just behind me. Then he was inside me, just slipped in like a well-shifted gear. He fit almost perfectly, though some part of him was larger than I'd been before. No one else would notice. After a while, I hardly noticed either. We walked around the garden, feeling each other's thoughts, dreaming of longer walks through wilder landscapes. So when our wife came home a little later we hardly noticed she was there, until she called out to us. She was two almost-identical people standing there, laughing and happy to see us. Both of her was walking out to meet me now, and I noticed she wasn't exactly the same as herself. They opened their arms for a kiss and I wondered which one was the solid one and which one was the ghost. We walked through each other, arms held out to hug; and then we tried again, and again, until we found ourselves as two solid bodies, and walked back into the house to cook dinner, pleased once again at the grace of our good luck.

Taint

It's been raining softly for so many days, mushrooms have sprouted up all over our back yard. I walk around with my mushroom book, trying to identify which mushrooms we might eat, though I give up before long, since so many of the pictures of the poisonous types look like the delicious ones, and who knows what we have here, so close to the tropics. As I'm wandering around in the rain, I notice the mourning doves landing on our back porch, eating the dry food—now soggy—we've left out for the half-wild cat we feed. They slide the bowl a bit further from the house with their beaks, as they coo appreciatively.

Yesterday, driving to the dentist, I worried about the fact that rain like this washes all our toxic chemicals into the bay: oil from cars and roads, fertilizers, insecticides and herbicides from our gardens and lawns. Small fish die off by the thousands when it rains for even a few days, though hardly anyone notices. I was nervous about the whole dental procedure I'd be undergoing—bolts drilled into my skull--which required I have many x-rays taken, that I swish toxic chemicals around in my mouth, that I bite down on molds that smelled like airplane glue. But what other options did I have? I'd rather not walk around gap-toothed and lisping for the rest of my life.

Afterwards I drove numbly home in a cocoon of relief that felt like happiness. I allowed myself to relax and recuperate all afternoon. The rain continued, which made it easy to sit inside reading and dozing. When Colleen came home from work she carried a beautiful bouquet of sunflowers for me, because she loves me and because she's a lovely person, and she made me chicken soup. Later that evening her skin started breaking out in hives like small bites all over her body, red welts that itched and bled when they were scratched. Was it something she'd eaten? Could it have been tiny bugs on the sunflowers? She searched her books of homeopathy to find a remedy that might give her some relief, but nothing helped. So she walked around the house wearing fewer and fewer clothes, scratching herself and muttering that scratching only made the itching worse.

By that time I was staring dumbly at the TV, having taken a painkiller the dentist had prescribed, though I'd been feeling hardly any pain. I took it just in case: to make certain I'd stay numb.

51

Any Shore by Dusk-Light

Another time, my father and I were swimming off our motorboat in late-summer Long Island Sound. The water was cold and choppy; the boat lurched wildly. We swam around trying to negotiate how we would climb back on. I was a good swimmer, but I was growing tired; even my normally unflappable father seemed to be getting worried as he tried to grab the mooring line to pull himself onboard. The line was too slimy to grasp; the boat was really pitching now. It seemed we might be knocked unconscious if we didn't watch out, and the shore looked dim in the dusk-light. Then, out of nowhere, a huge school of fish—bluefish perhaps—swam by, their bodies so closely-packed and solid that they bumped and pushed us roughly. By the time they had passed, the water was calm; they had dragged the calm water behind them. We climbed aboard without difficulty. My father took a blanket and wrapped us both inside it. We sat in that darkness panting and laughing. I remember the smell of that scratchy wool blanket—which reminded me of the wet smell of the chilly basement in the building we'd lived in years earlier, before my brother was born, down where the super kept his junk, where tenants could store things they didn't care that much about, in flimsy cages with combination locks. As a small child I'd imagined that if you walked farther back into that darkness you'd come across creatures as pale as the moon, who reached through their bars to touch you gently as you passed.

Other Forms of Dreaming

1.

He told me about a person whose legs wore away as he walked, until his torso met the ground and he could only stand there calling out and waving his arms until he got so tired he just lay down. Then as he crawled his arms wore away too. And then he just lay there breathing.

My brother told me then he could take me to this person, his old friend who lived in the grass. He told me we should bring gifts--shiny things were best, but old playing cards and pretty bottles worked too.

I must have misunderstood him, since all we saw when we got there was a circle of beaten-down grass with some trinkets in the middle: a broken watch, a china coffee cup. We sat there for a while in silence while the birds sang. Then, after we'd thrown our offerings into the circle, my brother showed me the hair that had been caught in the brambles, the small strips of cloth. He pointed up into the trees that were full of hunters' platforms, empty now until the fall, when the hunters would come again and fire from those trees. Sometimes they fired before they really looked, my brother told me, though they always shot to kill.

Another friend, he told me, sat down in the creek and melted away. He slipped from his clothes and his clothes were rinsed clean.

When we got home he opened his closet to show me, but the clothes had already been eaten by moths. They lay on the floor like ashes. My brother swept them up then. He sniffed them as though he could smell his friend there, and then he tossed them out in the yard. Nothing else in his closet had been damaged. He told me his friend had looked a lot like me. Then he reached out and touched my face like a blind person might have done, to see me by touching. It wasn't even dusk yet, so he closed his eyes.

2.

We were sitting in the garden, enjoying each other's company, drinking cool white wine, listening to the buzzing bees in the jasmine tree by the small pond filled with mosquito fish the size of a fingernail. We were talking about books we loved, places we'd visited, exuberant plans for the rest our lives. We were talking of old friends.

As we sat there, a beautiful black snake—a racer—slid from the wild coffee bushes. It slid between the legs of your folding chair and into the taller grass beyond the banana trees. It glistened in the afternoon sun as it moved. There were mourning doves and mocking birds and cardinals singing and fussing in the bushy trees. Next door someone sang as she swept her terrace. A butterfly landed on my hand and lingered there, tasting me. Soon you would get up and hug me goodbye, but for now the henna tree was blossoming so fragrantly I had only to breathe to be happy.

The Small Bones

I get up earlier than usual—the dark's still thick—and step out my back door, barefoot, onto the porch. I stand, almost naked, and listen, alert to the breathing and gradual waking going on all around me. I think of the creatures dreaming in the trees. My wife sleeps deeply, just the other side of the window, unaware that I'm out here listening. I love this quiet privacy, so different from the privacy of sleep. Yesterday I drove around the city looking for a doctor's office, getting hopelessly lost with each turn, until I miraculously found myself sitting in a bright little room, assured by the gentle but over-busy nurses that everything will be alright. Of course that can't be true, but of course I pretended to believe it. And pretending of that sort can sometimes work wonders. So now I stand here feeling a blush of gratitude for my body and for the life that's brought me to this place, so fragile and temporary and quietly urgent. All over the city, other humans are waking, groggy-eyed and reluctant. Soon the roads will be humming and the great machine will roll on, flattening the small grasses and saplings in its path, crushing the small mammals that sleep during the day, heading toward that cliff at the edge of the world, that plunge into ultimate darkness.

The Hungry Child

Walking in the woods on an autumn afternoon I found a hand-made ladder propped against an oak tree. I'd been walking by myself after many days indoors. The oak smelled delicious, musty and true, so I climbed that ladder up into the tree, whose leaves had turned leathery and brown. I climbed until I came to an old boat cushion wedged into a crotch, and a book sealed tight in a plastic bag. The book felt weighty and substantial in my hands. The plastic was opaque, so I couldn't see the title. It might have been a journal or a diary. After holding it a while, I left it as I'd found it. I climbed down through the tree as evening filled its canopy, and I walked home slowly along the familiar path. When I arrived at our house, my family was already in bed; they'd left my supper on the counter with a note explaining that we would be leaving very early the next morning, so I should eat quickly and try to get some sleep. I'd had no idea we were moving away, and I wondered for a moment whether I should wake someone to find out what clothes and books to bring, whether we'd know anyone where we were going, what kind of lives we thought we might live there. But the food looked delicious and I was very tired, and the kitchen was polished and gleaming with our absence, so I took my tray up to my bedroom with me and ate as slowly as any starving person can.

The Flood

*You're capturing something elusive, something
you're not always sure of, and you're trying to
capture it before it vanishes.*
                         --Philip Pearlstein

1.

During a lull in the rain, I took a walk to the marsh, just to be outside, and found a
bedraggled little dog running circles around a man who lay amidst a clutter of tide debris.
He wore an overcoat, shoes without socks, and refused help or money before I'd offered.
When he asked my name I remembered my parents and answered *don't have one*, then
asked about the dog: why was he so small; why didn't he bark? But the man said the runt
wasn't his, was just another kind of lie I hadn't learned to tell yet. He told me he didn't
have a name either, that he stayed too busy to indulge in such vanity. Then he turned away,
sighing, and fell back to sleep, and the rain resumed falling, even harder than before.

So I ran home, followed by that secret little dog.

By the time I arrived, the water had risen into the kitchen; my parents were lolling on the
floor, splashing each other and trying to teach my little sister how to swim. In the living
room my brother sat naked in water up to his chin and watched our brand-new color
TV, which seemed to work fine, even half-submerged: Another sort of miracle. The house
smelled of turkey and mashed potatoes, fresh-brewed coffee and apple pie.

Then my parents were doing the dead man's float, holding their breath so long that my
sister was quietly starting to cry. In another room the phone was ringing, so I waded down
the hallway to answer, hoping it would fall silent before I arrived.

2.

So much rain this year, she tells us, fish have started surfacing from their deep pools
underground, up through caves and coral and soil, into the puddles that are flooding our
gardens. When I wade through the back yard to the alley to dump the garbage, fish thrash

and splash me and sometimes cause me to drop the garbage bag, which they ravenously rip to shreds. Soon we may be swimming off our back porch. Then the rains will stop, as they always do in winter, and we will plant our garden, fertilized this year by the fish which will have died and rotted--unless they are able to slip back down into their underground grottoes. Pelicans and anhinga have landed in our oak trees.

3.

Do you feel the deep breaths that move through your body, she wonders, do you know who sings at the back of your head? My memory is faulty, but my hopes are eternal, like the foxes that set out at dusk. They dance and forage around our neighborhood while we're shut up inside eating dinner. And when I say *dance*, I mean it, she says: have you ever seen them jump for a bird which has swooped low to the ground, and catch it?

She tells us she understands music much more deeply since that afternoon she fell off the high dive while no one was looking, hit her head on a kick board in the water and went down. Now she knows harmony and dissonance as well as she knows how to chew her food; she knows all the words of all the jazz standards and even the most obscure operas, in their original languages. She says she doesn't even *like* that kind of music and starts to sing in other voices, back and forth, in harmony.

4.

We sat at the end of a concrete pier that stretched out into the St. Johns River and watched black skimmers circle, bottom half of their beaks zipping through the water, making a soft hiss, like gentle rain. In the grasses behind us, tall white birds stood still.

Years later we paddled kayaks out to a sand bar slung between two small islands where we could wade, watch birds, and gather shells. The water slapped from both directions, sending claps of small waves up into mist and breeze. We sat in the water there, rocking back and forth. Plovers flew near, rose up and fell into the waves, catching tiny food. A bedraggled pelican flew by, stabbing the swells but catching only water. High above, vultures and magnificent frigate birds moved in slow circles, almost out of sight.

58

5.

So I lie back in the water and look up at the sky and wonder what I would say to you if we met today as strangers living one of the many different lives we could so easily have entered, many times, with one of our other loves. I think you'd live in Colorado or California, and I might have ended up anywhere. We'd both be married, and I think we'd both have children--so our own children wouldn't exist, except as other people. Maybe we'd both be spending a few nights here on the beach on our way somewhere else. There'd be a summer storm and our sons, who would be about the same age, would rent boards and surf the larger-than-usual waves while we stood at shore's edge and watched. You'd have a pair of binoculars I'd borrow to watch them. I think I'd notice your eyes. Maybe your husband would be sleeping off a bad mood and maybe my beautiful wife would be having her fingernails painted again. Maybe I'd ask you to body surf with me, which you would demurely decline, since you wouldn't swim well; and maybe it would start raining hard enough to make the sand dance and our sons hoot with pleasure.

I see them out there now, floating out beyond the swells on their rented surfboards, laughing and yelling back and forth to each other with the same vivid energy that connected us, so many years ago. They don't even know each other's names.

Or maybe your son meets my daughter somewhere else, in another city where she's living for the summer while she studies anthropology, art history, simple food and love. Maybe he asks her to take a walk with him. It's beautiful there, walking at dusk beside that river, watching swallows scribble and dance.

Maybe they talk about their parents as they walk, or maybe they don't say anything at all.

--for Colleen

Evening Swim

My wife and I rode our bikes down to a park by the bay so she could take a swim. I sat on a bench reading while she climbed down the seawall, put her flippers on, grabbed her kickboard and kicked out. The water was calm, and since it had rained earlier that day, the surface of the water had that slightly fishy smell of salt water covered in a sheet of fresh rain.

As she kicked out, people taking walks after work along that short promenade stopped to watch her, asking questions—"is that a man or a woman?" "Is she swimming away?" "Should we call a lifeguard to save her?" I sat reading, pretending not to listen. It was a book about owls and the moon.

Soon enough she swam back in. I helped her pull herself up the wall, and we rode our bikes home through the evening, talking of the smell of the rain on that water, that still tasted fresh enough to drink. The water below that rain water was cold, and it was moving swiftly, she said. So I thought about fish and seabirds and owls. And by then, since it was almost fully dark, I thought about bats too, and I asked if she was chilly. "Only as chilly as wet grass," she laughed, "only as chilly as right now." I was going to ask what she meant by that silly statement but by then we were home, and there was dinner to be made...

Sunday Morning

We were reading a story about William Thompson, the English-born railway worker who feigned death while he was scalped by Cherokees, who lived to retrieve his scalp after it fell from a warrior's belt, put it in a pail of water and even tried to have doctors sew it back on his head. Before he died, many years later, he mailed that scalp to the Omaha library, and they put it on display. His hair is still healthy-looking and gleaming on its dried-up scalp. We were reading aloud about Witold Pilecki, the Polish hero who walked voluntarily into Auschwitz in 1940 and stayed for three years, documenting what he saw. We were reading that the oceans are rising more quickly than predicted. We were reading about the eyesight of swifts and kites, of hawks and eagles and crows. We were reading a review of that movie about the strange planet hurtling toward the earth, how the power would fail and cars wouldn't start and people would have trouble breathing. We were only half-reading about the music of Wagner's later period. Instead, we were reading about Susan Sontag's diaries, how grandiose and self-involved she was. We were skimming a review of a book about John Berryman, who was even more grandiose and self-involved; about sculptures in the snow that melt when the snow melts, whose melting is their truest form. Then we were reading about the vast rivers underground that gush out millions of gallons every hour. We were wistfully reading about a Japanese spa where we could drink small cups of green tea while we sat in a pool of warm water, being scrubbed or massaged, while the breeze fluttered the curtains which fell across the open door, to push them open wide enough for us to see the garden's rocks and sculpted waterfalls. We were reading small poems then, not quite haiku, of Basho and Dogen: *A snowy heron on the snowfield/where the winter grass is unseen/hides itself/in its own figure.* We were putting our reading aside and going out to putter in our garden, to listen to the cardinals and mockingbirds and mourning doves, to smell the spearmint we'd planted by the henna tree. It was raining then, softly, and we let ourselves get wet, soaked through to the skin, which belonged to us now.

The Moon Before Bedtime

This afternoon, I'm going to carry my yellow kayak down to the bay, where I'll slip it through the fence and slowly down into the water. Then I'll climb over the fence and down the wall to the barnacle and mussel-sharp rocks, step up to my knees in the sloshing water, and work my way into the boat. I'll push off and paddle slowly out to the bird sanctuary island in the middle of the bay, looking down into the water for fish or manatees as I pull myself along. No other boats will be out there this late in the day, so I'll let my thoughts roam. Maybe I'll stop paddling and drift. While I'm out there drifting, my wife will come home from work; she'll smell the soup I left simmering in the crock-pot. She'll change her clothes and go outside to our back yard, to see what's up with the small world we've planted there. As I paddle quietly around the island, tryAing not to startle the herons and frigate birds, the anhinga or the pelicans, she'll cut some garden arugula for salad, to go with the soup. Then maybe she'll call one of our children, both of whom live far away, or maybe she'll pour herself a glass of wine and wish she were out there with me, drifting back to shore in the brand-new darkness. She'll ride her bike down to that park and stand at the railing looking for my yellow kayak as it slides through the distance and approaches her there. And when I get out and dry off we'll sit on a bench in the park and drink a glass of wine and tell each other about our days. Then we'll go home for soup and arugula salad. After dinner we'll read, and just before bed, maybe we'll step outside and look up at the moon, a feather of light in the dark night sky.

*

Acknowledgements

Grateful acknowledgement to the following journals, where these poems were originally published:

CaKe: "The Tiny Grandma"
Ginosko: "The Night-Blooming Cactus,"
Hamilton Stone Review: "The Seed," "The Small Animals"
Mudlark: "The Purposeful Hum," "The Double Dream of Sleeping," "Sunday Morning,"

         "Windows, Mirrors, Chandeliers," "Solitude," "Duet," & "Living Without Names"
Origin: "The Flood"
Orion: "The Houses"
Pear Noir: "The Stranger's Continent," "No Such Thing"
Poetry East: "Until it Grows too Dark," "Ordinary Wonders"
Sisyphus: "The Moon Before Bedtime"
Sleet: "The Other Woman"
South Florida Poetry Journal: "The Animals" & "The Mushrooms"
Split Rock Review: "To Sing the World"
Swamp Ape: "The Shoes"
Yellow Medicine Review: "Forgiveness" & "The Hurricane"

"The Flood" appeared in an online chapbook entitled *The Flood*. (Floating Wolf Quarterly, 2011)

"Forgiveness" was made into a broadside by artist Lea Nickless as part of the SWEAT broadside project.

Parts of "The Hurricane" were excerpted by artist Laura Tan and made into a broadside for the SWEAT broadside project.

"Solitude" was made into a broadside by artist Tom Virgin as part of the SWEAT broadside project.

"The Flood" was made into a four-part broadside by artist Tom Virgin.

"The Hurricane" appeared in a limited-edition, handmade book entitled *Conversation Too*, produced in collaboration with John Dufresne, Yaddyra Peralta, Tom Virgin, Laura Tan, and Kari Snyder.

"Bones" was included in a limited-edition, handmade book entitled *The Ground Beneath Our Feet*, part of an art exhibition produced by WAIL (Word and Image Lab) in 2015.

"The Mushrooms," "Taint," "Satellites" and "The Gleaming" appeared in different form in *The Frozen Harbor*, by Michael Hettich (Red Dragonfly Press, 2017).

"To Sing the World" is for Jesse Millner, my first reader, best critic and brother-in-poetry.

Thanks to Carol Todaro for her beautiful cover image.

Thanks to Alan Davis, Silvia Curbelo and Mia Leonin for their generous blurbs.

Thanks to Tom Virgin for his friendship and collaborations.

Love and gratitude to Bob and Susan Arnold for many decades of friendship.

To Matt & Megan, Casey & Caitlin with love and gratitude.

To Colleen, the love of my life.

I am deeply grateful to Jay Snodgrass for his exuberant generosity, kindness and creativity, and for his wit and gentle heart--to say nothing of his boundless and self-effacing energy.

Many thanks to the Florida Division of Cultural Affairs for Fellowships in Poetry.

About the Author:

MICHAEL HETTICH was born in Brooklyn, NY in 1953 and grew up in New York City and its suburbs. He has lived in upstate New York, Colorado, Northern Florida, Vermont and Miami. He now lives in North Carolina in the shadow of the Black Mountain School. He has published over a dozen books and chapbooks of poetry. His work has appeared widely in journals and anthologies and he has collaborated with artists and musicians throughout Florida and nationally.

CPSIA information can be obtained
at www.ICGtesting.com
Printed in the USA
LVHW062225220119
604901LV00003B/334/P

9 780940 821088